# Demon Next Door

by Gordon Jacobson

# Contents

# Introduction

I spent seventeen years in law enforcement, working in two different cities in two different states.  I started in patrol, worked K-9, and ended my career in forensics, where I was certified as an expert in fingerprints and shoe impressions.  I was certified as an instructor in fingerprints, shoe impressions, crime scene investigations, and photography.  I taught crime scene photography for the Polaroid company and taught five different countries computer aided composites for the Federal Law Enforcement Training Academy.  The majority of my training were in FBI classes.

Before my time in law enforcement, I would spend time either with friends or by myself, looking for information about the occult.  It truly fascinated and scared me at the same time.  I was hooked on the stories I read and the stories I heard.  If someone told me of a haunted location, I would always go and see if I could have my own experiences.

Once I started my law enforcement career,  I would come across crime scenes and  calls that were out of the ordinary and either had hints of occult involvement or showed complete involvement.

The last seven years of my career I would see an increase in such calls.  It was my job the collect, photograph, analyze, and if needed, testify in court on my findings.

I realize that everyone has their opinion of evil, and for that matter, good.  There are differences in religious beliefs, as well.  I am not trying to change anyone's opinions or beliefs, I am just stating what I experienced.  I cannot begin to tell you how to feel about any of it.  I am not sure how I feel myself after all of these years.  Some things are beyond explanation.

I have not disclosed addresses or names.  Because of the nature of what I have written about, I am trying to protect those living that may have been related to those involved or still living in the house where the incidents happened.

I am sure those people do not want someone knocking on their door asking to walk around their house so they can experience the scene for themselves.  Believe it or not, there have been those who have done that.

Several of my friends for years have asked me to write down some of my experiences, so with this book I have done so.

These stories are not to be celebrated, as real people suffered, some dying.  I write them so you can understand what is out there, and what could be going on in your own neighborhood.

I want to point out that even though I mention satanists in some of the chapters, not all satanists practice what the ones I mention in the stories have done.  They will tell you they do not believe in human sacrifice, torture, child abuse, or anything else of a violent nature toward another human being unless it is to protect oneself.

Like all religions, there are a few outlying individuals who go to the extreme in their practice.  In so doing, we should not look at the religion as a whole to be that way.

An example would be in the christian religions, there have been several cases of child abuse.  But, the whole of the christian faith should not be judged by what a few individuals do within it.

Whether you agree or not, even those practicing satanism should be given the same respect.

I have made myself available to privately investigate cases for both individuals and government agencies, and do so on a semi-regular basis.  The only type of cases that I involve myself in are those believed to have some type of demonic activity.


*Gordon Jacobson*

# The House

I call this first story simply, *the house.*

This is one of the strangest investigations I was ever involved in, and one of the shortest. It was really over before it had much of a chance to begin. You will understand at the end.

I was on call this particular weekend. I was one of three officers that rotated for a week at a time to take calls after our normal working hours, which were Monday thru Friday, 8-5. We worked out of what was called the I.D. Section. We came out on calls that needed crime scene experts. Those calls would include burglaries, fatal traffic accidents, child abuse, rapes, and homicides, as well as anything else that the department felt needed our expertise. We were all highly trained and Federal Agencies would use us as well on Federal cases. I have testified as a fingerprint expert in Federal court for them, as an example.

I was driving back to my home from being called out one evening when I heard a call go out for a possible burglary in progress, and since I was close by, I radioed dispatch that I would go by and assist patrol in case I was needed.

Upon arrival at the residence, I noticed the patrol officer that initially was dispatched talking to an older gentlemen in the front yard.  I approached the two and the officer briefed me on their conversation.

Apparently, the gentleman with whom the officer was talking to, lived next door to the house that was the subject of the call.  He stated that the woman who had lived in the home had passed away and her funeral service had been earlier that day.  After the funeral, the family had given him a key to the house and had asked him to keep watch over the house until they figured out what they were going to do with the residence.  All the family members lived in other cities.  The gentleman agreed to do so, and the family thanked him and they departed.

Later in the evening, before dark, the gentleman went over to the house, went inside to make sure everything was secure.  He then left the residence, turning on both the front and back door lights, and then locking the front door.

Going back to his residence, he thought nothing more of his neighbors house and prepared dinner for himself, watched television until after the late night news was over, drank a last cup of coffee, and started to his bed.  That's when he noticed something strange.

Looking out his bedroom window, which faced the house he was watching, he noticed what looked like all of the lights were on inside the house!  How could that be?  He hadn't turned on any lights except for the front and back doors!  But, he was looking at the house and it appeared that every light was on.  Maybe there is a timer he missed?

He put on his shoes, grabbed the key, and he went next door to find out what was going on.  After unlocking the front door, he went inside and sure enough, every light in every room was on.  What in the world?  He made his way thru the house and everything was secure, nothing out of place, windows and doors were all locked.  He then started looking around for some sort of timer that would control the lights.  He looked everywhere he could think of, but could not find a timer.  He thought for awhile, then just told himself they were probably on and he just didn't notice.  Signs of old age, he told himself.  He made a round thru the house one more time, just to make sure everything was okay, checked all the windows and doors, then, after turning off all the lights inside, leaving only the front and back door lights on, locked the front door and went back to his house.

He settled in at his house, once again started getting ready for bed, it was nearly midnight by now, and happen to look out at the house again before getting into bed.

What the hell!  He couldn't believe what he was seeing!  All the lights were back on at the house! Someone must be playing a joke on him, he was not in a playing mood, so he decided to call the police, just in case it was more serious.

Now that I have brought you up to when I got there, we will continue our journey into what I believe is a very perplexing case.  Maybe you can figure it out.

The officer and I approached the house and made a walk around it, thinking we would find some signs of a burglary.  Neither one of use found anything, everything appeared to be secure.  I started thinking the gentleman may be right about a timer.  He
 had given the key to the house to the officer, so the officer then unlocked the front door and we cautiously entered.  It was pretty crazy, every light, and I mean, every light, was turned on.  I am talking about room lights, lamps, over the stove, EVERY light!  As we walked the house we were keeping our eyes on any type of timer, but I didn't have hopes for one considering the types of lights that were on.

The officer and I met up in the living room, after having made a thorough search of the house.  We both agreed the house was completely secure and we did not find anything that could cause ALL the lights to just turn on.  The officer asked me what I thought and I told him I had no idea.  He came to the same conclusion.  We then asked the gentleman that was watching the house to come in and take a look around to make sure everything was okay.  He looked around and said everything looked fine to him.  We all went thru the house turning all the lights off except the front and back door lights and left out securing the front door with the key.

We met up in the driveway and the officer was letting the gentleman know that as for now there was nothing we could do, but to call if he noticed anything else and we would gladly come back. The gentleman thanked us and was apologizing for wasting our time when I noticed it.

Are you kidding me? What is going on? The officer and gentleman heard me and when they turned around they saw what I was talking about. ALL THE LIGHTS IN HOUSE HAD TURNED BACK ON!

The officer and I looked at each other and yelled I would take the back and he grabbed the key and went into the house. I found nothing wrong in the back so I came back to the front and entered the house to join the officer who was making a search of the house. Nothing. Absolutely nothing! But, as we stood in the house, every light was on! We are obviously missing something! But what? We started another search of the house being very slow and methodical and checking everything we could think of. Breaker box, light switches, electrical outlets, under counters, behind furniture, EVERYTHING!

Then, while I was walking down the hallway that lead to the bedrooms, I saw something out of the corner of my eye that didn't seem right. Something about part of the wall. I called to the officer and asked him what he thought. He saw what I was seeing, although just walking down the hallway it was easily missed unless you were looking right at it.  A part of the wall seemed to be sticking out just slightly.  I started tracing the outline with my hand and it felt like it was some kind of panel.  I asked the officer if he had a knife on him, and he did.  He put the blade into the outline and after a few minutes a panel that was about four foot square popped out from the wall.  What could this be?

We both carefully placed the panel against the wall opposite of where we were standing and looked into what we had uncovered.

After shining our flashlights into the opening we couldn't believe what we were looking at.  We looked at each other with so many questions.  In front of us was a ladder.  Where it went we weren't sure but we were about to find out.

With weapons drawn, I followed the officer thru the opening and up the ladder to who knows where.  We climbed only about six feet or so and found ourselves in a room.  Looking around I found a light switch and turned it on. We were frozen!  We couldn't move!  I was in disbelief at what I was seeing!  I don't think we said anything for several minutes as we surveyed what was in front of us.

We found ourselves in a room about ten by ten in size, a pentagram was drawn on the floor in the color red with various symbols drawn around it.  One wall contained clothing that looked like robes.  Another wall contained several bottles of some type of substances, one bottle appeared to contain a blood like liquid.  There were bottles of liquor of various types, also empty glasses and bowls.  On the third wall there were different knives and swords hanging.  Against the final wall was a table with a black cloth draped over it.  Several candles were placed throughout the room both on the floor, tables, and shelves.  The candles were either black or red in color.  It gets better.  One of the candles was lit!

We both looked everywhere trying to find another entrance or exit from the room.  If there was one, we couldn't find it.  We talked it over and decided not to tell the gentleman anything about the room.  He was shook up enough about the lights, we didn't need to add this to his worries.  The officer would get in touch with his supervisor and find out how he needed to handle this and how he should write this in his report.  I would bring this up in the morning at the daily briefing the detectives have before going out on their cases.  After all, as far as we knew, no laws had been broken, people are free to practice whatever religion they desire, including the occult.  Many do this practice in secret, this room was certainly that.  The burning candle was a mystery, we extinguished it and left the room.  We secured the panel and turned off the lights and left the house.  We met the gentleman outside where he was waiting on us and told him we couldn't find anything wrong.  As we walked back to our cars the lights inside the house came back on.  The gentleman looked at us after noticing the lights again, and we told him not to worry it must be a special timer. He seemed to accept what we said because he went back into his house.

As we were about to leave the officer and I both heard what we thought was a voice. I couldn't understand what it said but it seemed to upset the officer. He told me to meet him at a convenience store before I went home.

I met him inside the store and he seemed to be shook up. I asked if he was okay and he looked at me and told me he didn't know. I asked him what he meant, and he said remember that voice we heard but didn't know what it said? I said I thought it was probably neighbors talking and he shook his head. He told me that he studied Latin as part of his Catholic faith. He said the voice we heard was speaking Latin. It said, "Don't come back!" I asked him if he was sure, and he said he was on his way to his church to get holy water! He was really shook up!

I thought about what he said on my way home and really didn't know what to think. I had known that officer for a few years and had never known him to lie or stretch the truth about anything before. And, I had never seen him so upset. Well, time to get home and some sleep before the next call.

The rest of the night was quiet so I ended up getting a decent night sleep. But I couldn't help dreaming about *that house*. As I was driving into work I was thinking about how I would address the morning briefing on the strange findings the night before.

At the briefing I waited my turn.  The reports from the night before are passed around to everyone so we knew what was going on and if we had any information or past experiences with the incidents, people involved, or locations.  We then speak on any information we have.  The process usually takes about an hour.

As it was getting close to my turn, one of the Detective Sergeants asked me if I had gone to a possible burglary call the night before.  I answered yes and that I was going to mention what was discovered when it was my time to speak.  He told me that I would probably need to return to the house after the meeting.  Puzzled, I asked him why.  He informed me that during the night after myself and the officer left it had caught fire and completely burned down!  My mouth dropped and I was speechless.  The sergeant asked me if I was okay and I responded that I would have to let him know later.

After the meeting I quickly drove to the house and discovered the fire department was still there.  One of the assistant fire chiefs was there and he was a good friend of mine.  I caught up with him and asked if knew the possible cause of the fire yet.  He said they were still looking but it appeared to be something that was in the middle of the living room.  What?  Middle of the living room?  I never saw anything on the floor in that room.

It was bare.  I asked him how?  He said still too early, but it was something in the middle of the floor.

As I was thinking about what he had just told me, and visualizing the living room from the night before, my friend interrupted my thoughts with a statement, 'you have to see this'.

He received my attention right away.  He told me to follow him which I did.  We walked thru what was left of the burned up house.  While walking I noticed something sticking up from the ashes.  As we got closer, I noticed it appeared to be some type of a figurine.  How odd, I thought to myself.  I had heard stories about items surviving fires, but never experienced that.  Usually when I get called to a fire, it is to process the scene because there is a death involved.  Processing and retrieving deceased individuals from a fire is challenging.  Anyway, as I approached the object I noticed it was about a foot tall.  When I was finally close enough to see what it was I was shocked!  In front of me was a statue of Baphomet!

I asked where was it found?  The chief responded right where you see it.

It looked totally untouched!  I couldn't see any damage to the statue.  I started to get my bearings of the house to find out where it was.  Of course, it was in the area of where the hidden room would have been.  I was getting nervous.  I don't know what type of person this lady was that had lived here before her passing and don't know how involved she was, if at all. But she had to be, didn't she? She lived in the house. I started looking around to try and find anything else from that room, but found nothing else.

The chief brought me back to reality by asking if I happen to be on the call the previous night to the house, I responded, yes. I then told him about the issue with the lights coming on after being turned off. He nodded and said they would look into that, but not sure how that would fit in with the fire starting in the middle of the living room floor. I hesitated telling him about the room, not sure how I would. I had been worried it had started by the candle we found still lit, but I know we put that out. Since he would see the police report the officer made, I decided to tell him.

After giving him the details he seemed lost in thought. I certainly didn't get the response I thought I would receive. He just looked at me and said okay. We never talked about that house again.

I went back to the station and went into my office and sat down. A lot to think about. My supervisor popped his head in and asked if I was busy with anything and I replied no, just needed to do a report on the house. He said perfect, do the report and have it on his desk by noon.

I finished the report and laid it on his desk by noon as requested. I then went to lunch. Afterwards I stayed busy and did so for the rest of the week. The following week at a moment when things were not so hectic, I went to the records department and asked to look at all the reports from that incident with the house. I did so out of curiosity on how the officer and fire department wrote their reports.  I was met by the supervisor of the records department who told me those reports had been sealed and were not allowed to be viewed by anyone.  What!  I can't even see the one I wrote?  She responded, no.

I left her department and went straight to my supervisors office to try and find out what was going on. He informed me that everything had been sealed and he wasn't able to tell me why, because he didn't know.  He agreed it was strange and unusual, but it was out of his hands.  He also was told to tell me to forget about it, and, DON'T GO BACK!

Those last words almost made me sick to my stomach.  What was going on?

I never found out.

In closing, I want to talk about some loose ends.  I will start with the gentleman who was watching the house and made the call to the police about, *the house*.  I found out later when the fire department was at the scene fighting the fire, he became ill and had to be transported to the hospital, where he later died.

My good friend, the assistant fire chief, a few weeks after this incident, fell ill with cancer and died.

The police officer who I met on the call, later resigned from the police department and went to work for the local catholic church.  He refused to ever talk about the incident.

And as far as myself, I went thru a divorce and a scare with cancer, but survived both.

As far as *the house* goes, I hear it is still a vacant lot.  I can't tell you for sure, because I didn't go back.  Never even drove on that street again.  I didn't want to think about it.

While I have been writing this story on my computer, parts of the narrative would disappear, go to bold print, the words would become mixed, just to name a few weird incidents.  Maybe someone or something didn't want me to write about it.

I was warned by other occultist whom I know, to be aware of what I was writing and to do a protection ritual.  Well, I forgot to do that until these strange occurrences started happening.  I then quickly did one and the problems seemed to have stopped.

With this case and all that happened, maybe you can tell me, *was there a demon next door?*

# Baby Sacrifice

This is a memory that I wish would just go away. Completely.  It is the bloodiest crime scene I ever had to work.  I want you to understand.  Blood was absolutely everywhere.  No matter where I looked, what I moved, there was blood.  Even the ceiling was covered in it.

I initially received the call as an infant death.  I assumed it was what is known as a crib death.  I hated to go on those calls.  The babies always looked like they were just sleeping and everything was fine.  Infants have a different color to them when they die, they look like porcelain dolls.  I would get so depressed after taking one of those calls and it would last for several days after.  This call, however, was more than that.  Much more.

The house I went to was in a lower end residential neighborhood known for burglaries and drugs.  Several of the houses were vacant.  This particular home had not been.

When I arrived I was met by the detective in charge of the case.  He told me it was bad, really bad.  I have been on some pretty bad crime scenes but when I entered this one I realized that the detective was not being truthful.  It was the worst one of my career.  I don't say that lightly.  When I was on call, I would average four to six bodies for that week.  I have seen a lot of death.

I like to familiarize myself with my surroundings when I get to a crime scene. I stop when I get out of my car and just take a nice slow look of the area. Get a feel of where I am, so to speak. It may sound ridiculous, but soak in the energy. It has always helped me in some fashion with my part of the investigation. I believe everything is energy and you can tap into that somehow. Depending on your beliefs and background, you may call it something different. My job is to capture, preserve, process, and photograph evidence to aid the investigators in making a decision on the crime and suspects, and if necessary, present that evidence as an expert in court. The rest is up to a jury and judge. I feel my job was done no matter the outcome. That is why I got along with attorneys from both sides, I just went with what the evidence showed me, nothing else.

Upon entering the home, I was overwhelmed. I have never seen so much blood. It was something out of a horror movie. As I scanned the room, I focused on an object on a table in the center of the room. What was that? As I made my way to it, being careful to not disturb possible evidence, I discovered what it was. A baby!

I found myself feeling somewhat dizzy for a moment, then regained my composure. This was going to be a long and rough day. Out of respect for the soul of that innocent child, I will not go into the horrible details of what she went thru in her last moments of life.  To be honest, I don't want to think about it enough to write it down.  I hope you will understand.  I know there are those who want every detail, I get it, but I cannot bring myself to write it down.  You will have to trust me, it was insane.  I almost did not include this story because of it.

Alright, back to the scene.  I started by photographing and video taping the room.  After completing those tasks, it was time to collect evidence.  I started with taking various blood samples from the room and body.  This took some time due to the large amount in the room.  Once that was done and properly documented and labeled, I moved on to any other types of evidence that may be present.  We found some sort of dagger near the body that was later proven to have been used in the murder.  I went on to collect other items, carefully ensuring their location was properly documented.

Among the items collected was a collection of books that all seemed to deal with occult themes.  The Satanic Bible appeared to have been well used, but the other titles looked worn as well.  I started to think this might be heading into a very dark direction.  There were other signs, such as candles in the colors of red and black, containers of salt, and jars of who knows what.  I was convinced we would find more once we removed the body and we started moving furniture.

So, it was time to remove the infant from the room.  I usually help with what is called, 'bag and tag'.  It is basically just putting the body inside a body bag and attaching a tag for identification for when it reaches the morgue at the pathologists office for an autopsy.  It is done with the greatest respect for the deceased as possible.  I have worked with a lot of people around the deceased and every person I have seen always gave this respect.  I am sure, as in all areas, there are some who do not give this respect, but thankfully the ones I worked with did.  In this particular case, the attendants from the morgue performed this important task and saved me from having to do so.  I was able to stand at a distance and watch, which was uncomfortable at best.

Once the body was removed, I went to work looking at the area under where the baby was.  The table that the baby was laying on appeared to be a regular end table you can find at any discount furniture store.  Draped over the table was some sort of cloth, looked like it was black in color, but it was hard to say due to the large amount of blood.      I collected the cloth and continued my search.  On the floor, under the table with the body had been laying, was drawn a pentagram with various symbols drawn within the circle and around the outside of it.  I had seen this before.  I shivered as I started taking photographs of it.  After completing this task, I was not able to find anything else of interest.  I then searched the living room again to ensure I didn't miss anything.  I do this by dividing the room in four sections, searching each section completely before moving to the next one.  I was able to locate a few other items that I collected as evidence that I thought might be needed and secured them.

The rest of the house then became my focus looking for evidence, taking photographs, and securing measurements for a later drawn diagram.  Nothing of interest was found in any other rooms except what I would assume was the master bedroom.  There I found additional candles and several books all that seemed to be based on occult themes.  The house overall appeared to messy with clothes strewn across the floor and several dirty dishes in the sink and on the dining room table.

When I reach the point that I believe I am finished with a scene, I contact the detective in charge, or one their supervisors, to give a briefing of what I have done and to ask if there is anything else that they may want or need.  It was during this briefing that I discovered that the two suspects, the parents of the deceased baby, were missing and that a search was on the way to find them.  They were known practitioners of satanism and the neighbors stated they pretty much kept to themselves.  Which, the neighbors preferred.  You never know what people are doing behind closed doors, even if you live beside them.  Maybe its better that way.

It took a few weeks but both parents were finally found. They were located in other states, if I remember correctly, one in Colorado and the other in Oklahoma.  Taking a few more months getting them extradited, they were finally brought back to our state for completing the investigation and prosecution.

Both parents eventually plead guilty and, as far as I am aware, are still serving their sentences in prison. They received life sentences, but, with our legal system, I am not sure if anything has been done to change that.  I hope not.

I am sure you are curious about the parents and why they would do such a horrible thing, especially to their own child.  Well, not sure if I can give you an exact reason, they were not clear themselves, often times dodging the questions with statements of their beliefs, but I will try.

Both of the parents had known each other since early school years.  Once in high school, their friendship turned into dating.  After graduating, they married. They appeared to have a happy relationship, both working good jobs, and eventually buying a home. After that, things starting turning a different direction.

It was revealed that they met another couple at a party they were attending and seemed to have a lot of things in common.  Both couples were successful and neither had any children but planned in the future to have a family.  The couples started hanging out with each other, visiting each other at their homes and going out to eat.  They were becoming good friends.  That is when things started to change.

The female suspect in this case, the mother, stated that the couple they met and had become good friends with, had suggested to them about participating in swapping partners for something fun and different. A new adventure, if you will. At first they hesitated, they had never thought about doing anything like that, they were devoted to each other and didn't believe in being with other people sexually. Both couples were very attractive and successful, and their new friends suggested that is what good looking and successful people do. Get it out of your system before settling down and raising a family, they said.

After a few weeks of them constantly talking to them about it, the suspects relented and told them they would try it, but only one time. They picked a weekend night and agreed that it would be at the suspect's friend's house.

The agreed upon evening came and the suspects went to their friends house. The female suspect stated she was extremely nervous, she had never had sex with anyone other than her husband. The female friend was very attractive and worried her husband might have more fun than she wanted him to. They had talked earlier and decided to just do the act and leave. They were to both find out it wasn't going to turn out that way.

They arrived at the friend's home and were greeted warmly. Upon entering the female friend hugged and kissed the female suspect and told her that they were going to warm each other up for the guys. She was totally surprised but could do nothing as the female friend started on her. They ended up having sex in the living room. Afterwards she was led into a bedroom with the male friend. Her husband was led into another bedroom with the female friend.

The female suspect noticed that the bedroom was lighted with several candles and the décor of the bedroom was in black and red. She was quickly pushed down onto the bed where the male friend ravished her. She stated that the whole time she was having sex with him he would be chanting. She didn't recognize the words he was saying and she didn't know what was going on but it seemed to drive him. After what seemed like hours he was done. They then went into the living room where her husband and the female friend were sitting on the couch having a conversation. She told her husband that she wanted to leave, but he acted like he wanted to stay. She told him she wasn't feeling well and wanted to leave. It wasn't really a lie, she was feeling sick in her stomach for ever agreeing to this and wanted to get back home. Her husband agreed and they said their goodbyes to their friends and left.

On the way home, the suspect's wife stated they got into an argument over their friends. She didn't want to associate with them anymore and didn't like the way the friend's husband had treated her in the bedroom. She wasn't comfortable being with another man because

she was married and she wasn't brought up to do such things.
She said her husband didn't see anything wrong with it as long as they did the swap with just those friends. They fell silent till they got home where she went and took a shower.

The suspect's wife said the friends kept calling them and wanting to get together again, which caused the suspect's to argue with each other. She finally agreed to one last time. She said it started the same way, but this time before going into separate bedrooms, the friends fixed them drinks and gave them a pill. They said the pill was to keep from getting a hangover. That was not the case.

After going into the bedroom, the suspect's wife noticed everything was set up the same way. The effects of the alcohol was starting to kick in and she also was feeling like the world was spinning but in a way that would make you sick. She was pushed onto the bed for another session with the male friend. He again was chanting and she felt there was someone else in the room but couldn't see them. It also felt like the friend got off of her and while she saw him in the corner it felt like someone else got on top of her and starting having sex with her. She remembered nothing else until the next day with she woke up in her bed at her house. She was glad she was not going to do that again. She would refuse.

When she got up and went into the living room she noticed her husband reading a book.  She asked what it was and he told her it was the Satanic Bible.  She asked where he got the book and why was he reading it and he responded that it was a gift from their friends.  Another argument.

To shorten this narrative, over the next few months she was slowly talked into doing rituals with her husband.  She was told it was to help them get more money that would allow them nicer cars, nicer house, go on trips, and on and on.  She loved her husband so she went along.  There was no more hook-ups with their friends and she was glad for that.  She found out she was pregnant, didn't know how that could be, she was always careful to take her birth control, but, there you go, those things happen.

They weren't ready for a family, but they were still excited.  Her husband was hoping it was a male and was always reading a new book on the occult.  Their friends seemed to be very concerned about her pregnancy and was always calling about how she was doing.  She thought that was strange.

When she was ready to give birth, the friends came over to do a ritual.  She wasn't sure about it, but they convinced her it was to make sure everyone would be healthy.  Knowing the friends were practicing satanist, she thought it odd.  She just thought they were into sex and drugs, but she found out, that wasn't true.

The child was born and everyone was healthy. The friends would often come by and check on the baby. She didn't say anything, but she believed her husband was still getting with the friend's wife. She was always touching him with they came over.

When the child was three months old, the friend's came over and wanted to set up a special ritual. It involved drawing a pentagram on the floor of the living room and setting up a table for the baby. Before that, they had drinks and she was given another pill. Before she knew what was going on, she was pushed to the floor and the male friend was having sex with her. His wife and her husband was also on the floor embraced in passion. The next thing she knew she was standing over her baby with a dagger in her hand and her friends and husband were chanting some unknown words. Her hands were guided down with force.

She screamed and didn't know what was going on but noticed everyone running around and telling her she had to leave and get out of town or she would be thrown in jail.

Now you are up to where I came in. I want to add that a complete investigation was started looking for these, 'friends'. Nothing could be found out about them. No records of them working anywhere in town. When the address of where they were supposed to have lived, and where the suspects stated they went to visit

them and more, well, that house is vacant.  Has been
vacant for over a year, according to the owner.
The house was searched, but it was completely empty.
Well, almost.  A black candle was found in one of the
rooms.  Interesting.

Investigators believe she was making up the story
she gave.  The story probably fueled by drugs and
alcohol.  Fooling around with the occult and got caught
up and while high did the crime.

I have been telling you what the suspect's wife
said about the whole situation, what about the husband?
He never said anything.  Nothing.  Just had that far away
look in his eyes.  Acted like a zombie when I saw him.

I purposely left out all names and locations.  No
one needs to go to these places and try to find out about
these people.  Something beyond what we understand is
going on here, leave it alone.

I, for one, believe the suspect's wife's story.  She
gave a lot of details, some of which I left out due to it
didn't really add anything.  Some of the sex details were
quite graphic.  She had a very scared look about her
when I saw her.  No, not scared about prison, I think it
was something else.  Maybe it was the drugs and
alcohol, maybe it was more.  I really don't know.

Maybe, she was afraid of the *demon next door!*

# Alone and Dead

This is somewhat of a short story, but one that never produced an answer.  Neither for the police, or for her family and friends.

I was sent to a residence in reference to a deceased person.  Upon arrival I was met by a patrol sergeant who gave me a short brief on the situation and advised me the detective in charge was inside.

Once inside I observed that this home was extremely neat and tidy.  Well furnished and had a fresh smell to it.  An odd thing to say, I know, when you know there is a deceased person inside, but that was what I sensed.

The body of the deceased, a female, was located sitting in a chair in the living room.  She was fully dressed and was sitting upright.  I thought that odd, because most I see are slumped over.  She was totally upright, just like she was still alive.  Her eyes were still open and starring at whatever those who have passed stare at.  I noticed a firearm in her right hand, which was resting in her lap.  I looked at her and noticed what appeared to be a single gunshot wound to her chest, in the heart area.  Very little blood was visible.

While talking to the detective, no signs of a break-in were found, so he was looking at a possible suicide. Much more investigation was needed before the final answer, but you do have to have a starting point. Homicide was not eliminated, just added to the many possibilities.

I processed the scene, and the whole time I couldn't help telling myself that this had to be one of the cleanest and most organized house I have ever been in. Most crime scenes are not near this clean and neat. Everything was in its place. Not a single dirty dish anywhere. The beds were made and no clothes laying about. The home was in a very nice neighborhood and even her yard was mowed and trimmed professionally.

I finished my part and after the deceased was taken care of and removed, I left to go back to my office and write my report.

After a week or so, I ran into the detective that was investigating the case and asked how it was going. What he told me left me shaking my head.

The investigator had talked to family, friends, and co-workers. They all pretty much said the same thing. She was well liked, no financial issues, no health problems, and no relationship issues. The house had no signs of a forced entry, and the firearm used matched the bullet retrieved from the body. The firearm was legally purchased and owned by the deceased. She had bought it a few years previous due to her living alone and just in case she needed it for protection.  She displayed no signs of depression and was not on any type of medication.  She was thirty-eight years of age and had never been married.  The condition of the house was normal, she was described as a very neat and articulate individual.  The family was just as perplexed as the detective in what could have caused her to take her own life.

The autopsy report did not help.  No signs of alcohol or drugs in her system nor was she suffering from any diseases.  The report stated she was a normal and healthy woman.  They were going to classify the death as suicide.

Both myself and the detective had been on multiple suicide calls and this one really stood out from all the rest.  In fact, she is someone I think about after all these years, it really bothers me not to know what happened.

When we both sat down to review the case, to see if we missed anything, we both noticed from the photographs that she was in a chair facing towards a hallway leading to the bedrooms in her home.  At the end of that hallway, there was a door that opened to a closet.  While searching the house we both saw that the closet was empty.  Nothing special about that, she is single and it was a big house, so she just didn't have anything to put in it.  It did seem odd when we were looking at the pictures that she seemed to be starring at the closet. She put herself in that particular chair and faced that particular door. Could mean absolutely nothing, I agree. Still, odd.

Why did she die? No one ever found out. She was the only one who had that answer. For whatever reason, an attractive, young woman, who had everything going for her, decided to kill herself. Makes no sense to me.

Maybe she knew something we didn't, did she have a *demon next door?*

# Voodoo in the Bayou

This case was my first dive into the world of voodoo. I learned so much about the inside workings and some of the people that live in that world. It would come to help me many years later as I dealt with the daughter of a high voodoo priestess in another state. Obviously, as you can figure out from the title, this case happened in Louisiana.

I was actually a patrol officer at the time of this case and still early in my career before moving and working as a I.D. Tech with another department in another state. It was the day shift and I received a call to go to a residence for a welfare check. Simply put, I needed to go and see if the person or persons were okay.

The original call came in from a bank where this person worked. It was a female employee that had not showed up for her scheduled work day and they were worried about her. They mentioned in the complaint that she never missed work. Several attempts to call her on the phone were not successful.

Her residence was located at the end of an unpaved road. The house was by itself with the next nearest residence at least a half block away. The first thing I noticed was the fence around the house. It was a basic chain link fence, but it must be at least ten feet

high!  I had never seen that before.  It gave me a sudden
thought that whoever lived here was trying to keep
something in instead of out.

As I got out of my patrol car another vehicle
drove up.  It turned out to be the daughter of the person I
was checking on.  She appeared worried and told me she
was glad I was there.  Fumbling with a set of keys, she
found one and put into the lock on the gate.  I thought it
was odd to have a lock on your gate, but I guess it went
along with the sheer size of the fence.  Once passed the
gate, it was a short walk to the porch and then the front
door.

This is where it started getting a bit more strange.
The daughter again fumbled thru a set of keys to find the
right ones to unlock the FOUR deadbolt locks.  While
she was unlocking the door, I casually asked why all the
locks?  The daughter replied that I wouldn't understand.
Okay, I thought to myself.

After the locks were opened, we went inside.  The
house was neat and clean.  The daughter went hurriedly
past me and toward what I found out later was a
bedroom.  I started in the other direction and found the
woman we were looking for in the bathroom, deceased.
I found the daughter and had her sit in the living room
on the couch and told her the news.  She obviously
became very upset and started crying.  I used the
telephone to call in what I found and asked for a
supervisor and for the coroner.

I turned my attention back to the daughter to try and comfort her as much as I could.  I explained what would happen next and asked her if their was anyone I could contact to come be with her.  I really didn't think she should drive after the news she had just received.  She told me that she was fine and that she just needed to soak in the reality of her mom passing.

I did a quick search of the house and everything seemed to be normal, no damage, no signs of a break-in, everything normal except that every room had a clove of garlic placed on a table.  After the search I asked the daughter if her mom had been ill, and she replied no.  I then asked about the garlic and she told me that her mom was trying to protect herself.  She went on to say, it obviously didn't work.  I became interested in that last comment, and asked her what she meant.  She took a deep breath and told me her mom was a priestess in a voodoo group.  She got into an argument with another priestess from another group and became worried.  Continuing, she stated the other priestess was powerful, more than her mom, and word was out in the community that a curse had been placed toward her mom.

I sat back and had to think about this.  At this time in my career, I had not had much experience with any parts of the occult, including voodoo.  I had heard people talk about it, most of it with fear, and I use to go with friends to supposedly haunted places, but never *actual* experiences.  While I was still processing what she had just told me, my supervisor and the coroner arrived.  The coroner did his work and had the body taken away to his office.  He talked with the daughter briefly, then left.  I told my supervisor what I had learned so far, and he just nodded.  Didn't seem to surprise him what I said to him.  He asked the daughter to come down to the police department for a quick interview with a detective and she said she would.  The house was then secured and we left.

At the station the daughter was taken into an office to talk and give a statement to a detective.  I was also allowed to sit in on the interview.  The first part of the interview went over the information that I was given at the house.  The following was additional information given by the daughter during the interview.

The daughter said that her mother had been into voodoo pretty much all her life.  People would come to her with problems ranging from health issues, relationships, money, and missing persons.  Other issues, such as curses, her mom would stay away from. But, within the last year or so, her mom started doing workings in a darker part of voodoo, mostly because she needed the extra money that it brought in for her.  That is where she started having problems with another voodoo priestess in town.  Before, she was the only one who worked the dark side, and now, her mom started which took money away from her.  The other priestess warned her to stop, but her mom thought she was strong enough to not be affected by any curse she sent her way, so she continued.

I had experience before this case, with another situation that involved voodoo.  I found myself working the overnight shift and went into a small cemetery at the end of a city street.  I was curious about this cemetery, I had never been in it, and so I decided to take a drive thru.  It only had one way in and the same way out.  The road inside the cemetery was just a small dirt drive.  While I was driving, I noticed that one of the graves had been opened, and not only that, a human skull was sitting on top of it.  For those not familiar with Louisiana, it is common for the graves to be above ground due to the high water table.  For those buried in the ground, they usually have a cement vault put in to prevent the casket from breaching the ground.  I have seen old graves that were buried without a vault and you can see parts of the casket poking out of the ground.  This was an above ground grave, with the grave being built out of bricks with a cement slab top.  The brick work was damaged and bricks moved, exposing the casket.  The skull of the deceased that was resting in this grave was what I found sitting on the slab top.

When I discovered this, I radioed my supervisor and he told me to meet him at another location.  Meeting up with him, he advised me that we didn't bother with that grave or cemetery because it was taken care of by the community that lived around it.  The skull was that of a man that lived many years ago and was thought to be a special person in the voodoo religion.  Every month someone would take the skull from the grave and use it in whatever ceremony they did, and then they would return it.  They placed it on top of the slab to show it was used, and then the maintenance people for the city would place the skull back into the grave and position the bricks back in place.  I never went back to that cemetery again.

I wanted to give you this information because it ties into this particular case involving the death of this woman.  I am a big believer that what you may experience today, may be significant in the future, whether tomorrow, or years away.

Now, back to the interview with the daughter. She mentioned this cemetery and the skull.  It seemed that this skull plays an important part in doing the darker rituals, and her mom was using it when the other priestess demanded it.  Her mom said she was busy with it.  This apparently made the other priestess very angry and told her mom that she was messing with the wrong person and that she will find out the hard way what that meant.

This seemed to frighten her mom.  She started doing all kinds of protection spells and put the garlic in every room of her house for added security.  She added the locks on her front door and put up the fence around her house and blessed the boundaries with chicken blood.  She had asked her mom if all that was necessary and she replied that she had seen that priestess do some very high magic, she felt she was very powerful.

This incident between the two ladies had happened over a year ago, so the daughter had thought everything had settled down.  But lately, her mom seemed preoccupied and tended to be looking over her shoulder constantly.  When she asked her mom what was bothering her, she just said she saw the 'black' dog following her.  When asked what that meant, she said it meant death was following her, and she felt it was from a curse.  That conversation had taken place just a week ago.

The detective asked if she knew the name of the priestess her mom was talking about, the daughter said no, but she knew her 'magic' name.  The detective wrote it down and then thanked the daughter for her time and was sorry for her loss.  He also stated he would try and find this priestess and get her side of the story.  The daughter thanked him and told him to be careful, especially if he didn't know anything about voodoo.  She then left the office.

The detective turned to me and said I guess we now try and find the priestess.  He went back to his office and picked up his phone and started calling around to see if he could get that information.  It didn't take long, she apparently is well known in some circles, and we were on our way.

The neighborhood we were going into is in a run down part of town.  Nearly all the homes are in need of some type of repair.  I was curious what the house

looked like that the priestess lived in.  It didn't take long
to find out.

Her home was simple, but appeared to be well
maintained.  The yard was neatly trimmed, and
everything about it seemed, tidy.  I wondered what type
of reception we would get when we knocked on the door
and identified ourselves.  I was surprised.

While approaching the front door, it opened.  We
were warmly greeted by a women in her early 60's
whose smile showed she was not upset, at least on the
outside, that we were there.  She welcomed us into her
home without asking why we were there.  After being
seated in her living room, she asked if we needed any
refreshments, which we graciously declined.  She seated
herself and continued to smile at us, as if saying, you
first.

The living room was neat and clean, and was
furnished with older, but very nice, furniture.  It also had
an unusual smell.  Not offensive, but different.  I
couldn't quite place it.  Then it came to me, I remember
that smell from the woman's house that had died.  I
quickly looked around and found that this priestess also
had cloves of garlic placed on a table in the room.  I
would guess I would find them in all the rooms if I
looked.

The detective spoke first and told the priestess
why we were there.  She listened intently while he
relayed all the information.  She smiled the whole time.

After the detective finished, she seemed to take a few moments before replying.  She admitted to being a voodoo practitioner and admitted to helping people when they came to her, but only within the convenes of her religion.  She denied taking or using the skull from the cemetery, but knew about it.  Her practice was strictly for healing, and, yes, she knew of the deceased woman, but not on a personal level.  No, she would never put a hex or curse on anyone, or even try.  She didn't know if she knew how to do that.  Yes, she had heard of people doing those things, but it wasn't within her realm of practice.  An offer from her to do a quick negative cleansing for us was turned down.

In short, we got nowhere.  While we were getting into our vehicles to leave, I looked back at the house and noticed her waving to us with that amazing smile.  While driving away, I turned and looked again and saw her still standing in front of her door, but it seemed like the smile was gone, and a look of what I could only describe as hate.  Seems strange to say that, but that is the best way to rely how I thought.

Weeks went by and I was doing my job as a patrolman and hadn't heard anything else.  I happen to see the detective that was in charge of the case and asked if anything had changed.  From what I knew, there wasn't really anything that could be done.  How do you prove a curse killed someone, and how do you charge a person who may or may not have put that curse on the person.  Someone else would have to figure that out.

He told me that the autopsy report had come back and it didn't give any information other than the woman appeared to have died from natural causes. The only remarkable item noted in the report was both of her feet had a small burn mark on each heel. The pathologist could not explain what they were, but he was sure they had nothing to do with her death. The case was then closed due to lack of evidence of a crime.

Months went by and many other situations to take care, I learned a few more things about this particular case. The detective had gone back to the house for follow up questions. He found that the priestess no longer lived there. He asked the new occupants of where she could be found and they replied they didn't know. He then went next door to ask the neighbors of her whereabouts and they were visibly shaking when he mentioned her name. They begged him to leave and not mention her name again.

He never did find out where she moved to, and he never heard of her again. He reached out to the deceased woman's daughter to try and find out if she had heard anything about the priestess's new location, and she replied that no one she knew would talk about it. They were afraid of her abilities. He then told her about the burn marks on her mother's feet, the daughter screamed and hung up the phone. The detective was never able to locate or talk to her again.

After a few years went by, and before I moved to another state to work for another agency, I drove one last time to the small community cemetery. As I drove past the grave of the man whose skull was being used in voodoo rituals, I saw it setting on top, once again. Apparently, it was still being used by someone, maybe even the priestess who disappeared.

If you are living in Louisiana, she may be, *the demon next door!*

# In Plain Sight

In continuing along the voodoo theme, I will tell you of a personal experience that happened to me after I retired from my law enforcement career and had started my business endeavors. It's another short story.  I hadn't pushed aside my occult work, I still gave help and information to those who needed the knowledge I had obtained thru years of experience.  And, on occasion, investigated claims for both public and government entities.  It wasn't ghost hunting, I went darker and for the real thing.  This particular episode occurred while at work in my new career.

There was a young woman who worked for me and always had a big smile and a laugh that was contiguous.  She had been with me for nearly a year when she told me she was waiting for the man of her dreams to appear.  I told her I hope he shows up and I think there are probably lots of women with that same thought.  She just smiled and laughed. She started telling me that she had been busy at home and spending long hours doing a project that she had hoped would bring her something special.  I replied that I hoped it worked for her.

During this time I had noticed that the quality of her work was going down.  She was also starting to show up late for work.  She had not been like that before, so I was growing concerned.  I mentioned to her my concerns and let her know she could not continue and I would need to see improvement.  I know she was better than what she was doing, and I was worried for her.

Looking down at the floor, I gave her some time to think about what she needed to say next.  She then sat up and said, okay, I will tell you.

Her mom was a voodoo practitioner and had been teaching her the path.  One of the things she was teaching her was how to get a man.  She had someone that she had a lot of interest in and had taken his picture and printed a copy of it.  The picture was then placed under one end of a floor rug, and she would walk back and forth over it chanting a spell to bring him to her.  This took several hours, including during the night.  That was why she was coming to work tired and was having difficulties doing her job properly.  I looked at her, not with disbelief, I knew from experience that she was probably telling the truth, but with surprise.  I didn't have any clue that she would be the type to practice voodoo, not that I could tell you a type, she just didn't seem someone who would.

After taking this in, I asked her if it was working.  Yes, she said, I have a date with him this coming weekend.  I told her I was glad, but did it now mean she would get enough sleep to be able to do her job properly?  She replied yes, and apologized.  The next thing she said stunned me.

Please don't be mad at me, I felt I had no choice, she started.  Pulling at her pants pocket she pulled out three items and laid them on the desk.  I immediately recognized the items as belonging to me.  I looked at her questioningly.  In my practice, according to my mother, I had to posses three items of yours on my person to keep you from firing me from my job.  By having these items meant that I could control your feelings as they pertained to me.  All I did was to make sure you wouldn't do anything as it concerned my employment.  Now that my situation is completed, I can return these to you as I don't need them anymore.  Again, she said, I am sorry.  She then stood up and left the office.  I was speechless.  There were no words that I was able to form to say anything.

Weeks went by and everything seemed to return to normal as far as the work environment was concerned.  She was back to being her old self and very productive at work.  I was always a little apprehensive when I had to be around her, not knowing what she was thinking or doing.  She just gave me that smile.

About three months after all this first started, she came to me and put in her two weeks notice of leaving my company.  The reason she was leaving was the fact that she was getting married.  To who, you ask?  You guessed it, the man she had worked a spell to get.  I gave her my congratulations and best of luck speech.  One her last day, she said I really needed to go to a fast food restaurant that was located on a side of town I never visited.  Go to the drive-thru, someone wants to say hi.  I just looked at her like why would I do that?  I didn't know anyone who worked there.  That was the last I have ever seen of her.  I do wish her well.

I will admit what she last said for me to do had been on my mind for several weeks after she had left.  It seemed a weird thing to say.  I racked my mind trying to figure out if I knew anyone that had gone to work for a fast food restaurant.  I could not think of a single person.  Doesn't mean that I didn't miss someone, I certainly cannot remember everybody.

Well, as you can guess, my curiosity got the best of me and one afternoon I took a drive.  I found the fast food establishment fairly easily.  I am not that familiar with the part of town it was in, but I came across it quickly.  I found myself going to the drive-thru lane and making a small order.  I waited my turn and as I made my way to the window to pay and pick up my order, I heard voice say my name and that they were glad to finally meet me again.  Again?  Leaning out of the window was an older woman with a big smile and an easy way about her.  I asked her do I know you?  She smiled and answered yes, and no.  She gave a loud laugh and told me not to worry, my future life held many successes and to enjoy every single one as if was my last.  I looked at her for what seemed to be an eternity, I caught myself and apologized, thanked her, and drove off.  There were several cars behind me so I couldn't very well start a conversation with her without holding up other customers.  I could still hear her laughing as I driving away.  That smile, where have I seen that smile?

As I was driving away from that restaurant, it came to me where I had met that woman and where I remember that smile from.  I pulled over and had to think.  I felt I was losing it.  Can't be!  Spending a few minutes getting myself together, I pulled back into traffic and went home.

Have you figured it out?  If not, let me tell you….the older woman who waited on me at the fast food restaurant….I swear she was the high priestess I had met in Louisiana all those years ago….I am convinced!  That smile, I will never forget it!

I asked myself, was there a *demon next door?*

# Recruit

I had been working for a few years in the I.D. Section of my department and gotten to be good friends with the detective who mainly worked occult crimes. When he received one of those cases, and he had evidence to collect, preserve, or photograph, I was always requested. When he called my office or came by, I knew I was about to go on an adventure. This case was no different.

He gave me a briefing on this new case he had been assigned. He figured he would need me because he understood there would be several items to document and collect. I didn't have anything needing my immediate attention so I advised my supervisor of the situation and then left with the detective to go to the scene.

In the office I was told this was a case of a young male subject trying to recruit people into his coven. He was promising wealth and material things in exchange for them 'giving' themselves to the dark side. The complaint came from a concerned parent about her daughter. It seems the daughter was excited about being in this new group and was arguing with her mom about finding a job. She had just graduated from high school and her mom said she needed to help out with the bills. The daughter was saying she didn't need a job because she would be getting money from this group she had joined.  She could do whatever she wanted because she was going to be taken care of.  She even went so far as to promising to buy her mom a new car.  The mother didn't believe anything her daughter was saying and became concerned about this 'group' her daughter had found herself being a member.  The mother had also noticed her daughter wearing new clothes and jewelry.  When she asked about that, the daughter replied I told you I was being taking care of!

The detective did try to interview the daughter, but she refused.  So, after some checking, getting some tips from informants, he was able to locate the house that this group met and the name of the young man who was the supposed leader.  He was also able to secure a search warrant for the premises.

Arriving at the residence, which was located in an older part of town, but still a good neighborhood of well kept homes, we were met at the door.  It was a young man, maybe late teens, early twenty's, with a pleasant face and stated, I was wondering when you would show up.  The detective and I gave each other a glance, and then introduced ourselves.  The detective showed him the search warrant and the young man stepped aside and said that we didn't really need, one, we were welcome.

Upon entering the home, it appeared to be a nice and neat older home.  Nothing fancy inside, just basic furniture, enough to be comfortable.

The detective advised him why we were there and asked him what he knew about what we were hearing about him.  He invited us to have a seat and he told us he would answer whatever questions we had.

The first question involved whether he was part of a group or anything like that.  He responded he wasn't sure what he was asking, but he was a practicing occultist, if that is what he wanted to know.

Next question from the detective was if he knew of a certain young girl, he provided the name of the complainant's daughter, and what part she played within the group.

The young man responded that the group was really a coven, so he could start referring to it as that, if he wanted, and, yes, he knew the girl.  She was the newest member.

She seems to under the impression, according to her mother, that you will supply her with all the money she needs so she won't have to work.  She also is wearing new clothes and jewelry, which is making her mother worried about what she is doing.

Of course, replied the young man.  We worship the deity, Baphomet.  In doing so, he brings to us wealth and material things that we desire.  All we have to do is give him our attention and provide him with our abilities to please him.

That is all there is to it?, asked the detective.  Is that how the girl got the money and clothes?  Just do a ritual or something like that?

"Something like that", replied the young man, "she had to show she was willing to receive the blessings".

"Have sex with the coven, of course.  How else can you show your willingness to give?",the young man responded.  "Don't worry, I made sure she was at least eighteen, as I do with all members," he added.

"You paid her to have sex.  That is what it boils down to," stated the detective.  "No magic involved in that."

"You are not understanding," replied the man, "you have to give to receive."

He then lead us to a bedroom that had been converted to some sort of a ritual room.  In the room was the standard pentagram drawn on the floor, with various symbols written around it. Various candles located all over the room.  Assorted books, and small cups, green in color placed around the circle.  There was also a small statue of the demon, Baphomet.  The room also had a bad stench.  Reminded me of urine.  What had they been doing in here?

The man started, "this is where we do our ritual and give thanks.  We read and study, then we give of ourselves so that we may have. We urinate into the cups, then pass them around so everyone has a chance to drink of our bodies, then we engage in group sex to prove we are united and are willing to give to receive."

Myself, along with the detective just shook our heads. We had investigated a lot of occult related cases, and neither of us had ever heard of this. Sounded like a scam just to get sex from unsuspecting individuals looking for an easy way to get things. Even those who are authentic practitioners of the occult, which that could be anything from wiccan to satanists, and everything in between, they will tell you nothing comes for free. You have to work for it and towards it. You can't sit on your backside and ask Satan or whoever, to bring you whatever and he does. It does not work that way, and anyone who tells you it does, is scamming you, like this young man.

We finished up the interview and I took pictures of the house, and in particular, the ritual room and items within it, and we left.

Back at the department, the detective and I talked about what we discovered. We both agreed he was not a true occultist, just someone trying to impress others in order to receive sex from them. The detective was going to call the complainant and let her know what we found. He also wanted her to bring her daughter to the police department so he could tell her exactly what type of situation she was in. He couldn't force her to come see him, but he made sure her mom made it clear it would be something she would find in her best interest.

The next day, both the mom and daughter arrived at the police department.  I was allowed in the discussion, and I also brought enlargements of the photos I had taken.

Mom was nervous and was visibly shaking. Daughter, on the other hand, was looking like she didn't want to be there and her face was stiff.  This was my first time seeing her, and she was a very beautiful young lady.  Tall, blue eyed blonde with a nice figure.  I could see why the young man wanted her in the coven.  I assumed the other members matched the looks of this one.

The detective started by saying we had found the house and had talked to the young man who lived there. The daughter appeared not to have liked this revelation,S and at the same time I had noticed a slight nervous twitch to her lips.  He continued that we had taken pictures of the house, including the 'ritual' room. He then instructed me to bring out the photos and lay them on his desk so both mom and daughter could see them.  Mom was horrified and the daughter was outwardly showing signs of breaking down.

"You do know that this man is a scam, don't you?", asked the detective, toward the daughter.  "You have money, clothes, and jewelry because he paid you to have sex with him and whoever else.  You are not going to get any more unless you go back and do the same. No sex, no money. It is just that simple. Sit back and think about it. When you are ready, I will listen. When he gets tired of you, there will another." The detective told this in an even tone to the daughter. He then motioned to me to go out of the room and leave the mother and daughter alone to talk, if they wanted, in private.

He gave around thirty minutes before returning to his office. After taking our seats, the detective asked if anyone had anything to say or had any questions to ask. It was obvious the mother had been crying. There was a moment or two of silence, then the daughter responded with a desire to talk.

She started by saying she had met the young man at a party. He seemed nice and had an easy way about him. She was comfortable talking to him and did so most of the evening. They exchanged phone numbers and agreed to chat more in the following days. It had been nearly a week before she would hear from him. He invited her to his house for a get together with a small group of friends. She agreed. Upon arrival at his house, he warmly greeted her and introduced her to his friends. She said there was seven of them. All of them were males except one other female, which made her feel more relaxed. Later, she found them to be members of his coven.

The night progressed with no incidents and everyone was really friendly towards her. There was drinking and some drug use, but nothing excessive. At around midnight, they invited her into a room, which she found out was the ritual room. They told her not to be nervous, it was something they did in secret and helped them obtain anything they wanted. She was interested, she really didn't want to have to get a job like her mom was pressuring her to do. The other girl there told her the money was easy and she could buy whatever clothes she wanted. She had noticed everyone was dressed in the latest styles, and that was expensive. More than what she could afford. She was really interested.

The other girl moved next to her and put her arm around her. She started rubbing on her and kissed her cheek. All you have to do is give of yourself. Its fun and easy. Just give yourself.

The alcohol and drugs were kicking in and the daughter felt like she was in a dream. She felt the girl move her hand down to her buttocks and start to caress her. She didn't know how to respond. The girl then pointed to five one hundred dollar bills laying in the middle of the circle. She told her she could have them if she could have her. Give of yourself, so you can have.

Next thing she knew she was being lowered to the floor within the circle and hands were taking her clothes off. The girl was the first to have sex with her, then all of the guys that were there had a turn with her. She couldn't remember anything else and woke up in a bed with the young man. She quickly got up, found her clothes, and left the house. When she got home she took a shower. While undressing for her shower she felt something in one of her pockets. It was five one hundred dollar bills.

After a few days, she didn't know what to do. She was thrilled to have the money, but she was uncomfortable at how she received it. In fact, she didn't know if what she remembered happened, really happened.

Looking down at her phone she saw a text from the young man. He was asking how she was and if she wanted to come over for another small party. She was reluctant, but he had followed up with another text about how easy money was to get, and she should go shopping and spoil herself. There was more for the asking.

Reluctantly, she decided to go back to the house. Her mother had been constantly telling her to get a job and so that is what pushed her to go back.

Back at the house it was the same group of people and they welcomed her like nothing had happened the week before. She had told herself she was going to only drink a little and no drugs. At midnight everything started up again as it had the week before. She thinks they drugged her drink when they saw she wasn't taking any of the drugs. The girl started in on her like before

and she tried to move away from her, then everything
went blank.  She remembers nothing.  She woke up
again, naked, in bed with the young man.  She again got
up, dressed, and left the house.  That had been last week.

The detective asked her if she wanted to press
charges against them, and she replied no.  She just
wanted to forget it happened.  He told her it could
happen to someone else.  Shaking her head, she said I
don't want to do anything.

They finished up by the detective telling her if she
changed her mind to call him.  She said that she would.
She and her mother then left.

The detective called the prosecutors office to see
if there was anything he could do without the girl
making a formal complaint, and they said, sadly, no.  He
wasn't ready to give up on the case, so he reached out to
the owner of the house, which happened to be the young
man's aunt.  We figured she probably didn't know what
was going on with her nephew and her house, and that
might be a way to stop this nonsense.

After finding her, we went out to her house.  I was
taking the photos I took to show her.

The aunt was a handsome woman in her mid
seventies, widowed, and living alone.  She greeted us
and invited us into her home.  The detective started
explaining why we were there and was hoping she could

help us.  She appeared startled, and asked what could she possible do to help?

While the detective was explaining the situation, I started showing her the photographs.  She appeared to listen intently while viewing the photos.  Upon finishing, she politely looked up from the photos, handed them back to me, and said she didn't know how she could help.  It was out of her hands.

We both looked at each other as if to say, she couldn't have heard what was said nor the photographs!

The detective asked her what she meant by that, and she responded that her nephew was involved in something that had been in the family for generations.  She was the one that taught him!  She stood up and motioned for us to follow her.  We went down a hallway and stopped in front of a door.  When she opened the door, there in front of us was a ritual room almost identical to her nephew's!

She was quick to say that what they practiced was protected by freedom of religion.  She then handed the detective a card.  It was the business card of her attorney.  Call him if you need more information.  She then showed us the door and we left.

Back at the office the detective called the prosecutors office with what we had found out with the aunt.  They told him to be careful and if he tried to do any arrests on this case, to be in partnership with them,

and it had better be an air tight case.  They were aware
of the aunt.  She was wealthy and her friends were
people like the governor, mayor, and ceo's of many
companies.

I never heard anything else in relation to this case,
and as far as I was aware, no arrests were ever made.

You never know when you will find a, *demon
next door!*

# What the Dog Saw

Another short story, and not necessarily demonic, but it was an interesting experience.  It gave me another reason to try and understand what happens after we die. I know we all have our ideas, some based on our beliefs and religious upbringings, but to *really* know.

I received this call at around two in the morning. I was sent to a residence in reference to a deceased person.  Upon arrival I was met by a patrol officer, a supervisor, and a medical examiner.

They gave me a briefing on what they had.  A family member had been trying to get in contact with the deceased all evening.  At around midnight or so, they were starting to get worried and decided to go to the residence to make contact.  They couldn't get an answer at the door and they could here the deceased's dog barking.  They then decided to call the police.

The deceased had a history of medical issues, so her death was not unexpected.  I would normally not be called to this type of a case, except the family wanted the police to made sure nothing else could have happened to her, that it was indeed, a natural death. Because of that reason, I was called in.

The police officers had already searched the inside and outside of the house and found no signs of a burglary, or forced entry.  The medical examiner had viewed the deceased's body and had not found anything that would lead him to believe that she had not died from anything other than natural causes.

I took my photographs of the scene and got prepared to help the medical examiner remove the body from the house.

The dog that belonged to the deceased, was outside by the glass patio doors barking and watching us the whole time we were there.  It had been in the house and the officers had put it outside because of the barking and that it was constantly getting in the way.  I am sure it did not like all the strangers in it's master's house and wanted everyone gone.

Here is where the strange part comes in.  The medical examiner and I were getting together on our reports and he stated he was going to mark the time of death.  She obviously had been dead before we got there, but we have to put down a time that she was officially declared deceased.  When he gave me the time for my report, we both looked up at each other.  Then, we looked toward the dog.  When the medical examiner had  told me the official time of death, the dog had stopped barking.  When we looked toward the dog, it was looking straight up into the night sky.  It stayed like that for a few seconds, looked back at us, then slowly walked to a dog house located in the back yard, and laid down.

What was the dog looking at?  Was it the spirit of his master?  The medical examiner and I looked again at each other and he just shrugged.  We completed getting the body ready and had her transported from the house.

Again, not a demonic story, but more of a sad one. I believe the dog saw his master and she told him goodbye and he understood.  There was no use in barking at us in order to protect the house, the master was no longer there to protect.  He went to his dog house and waited for what the future had for him.

# Business Havoc

As I mentioned earlier, after I retired from my job in law enforcement, I went into private business. This story takes place at a business I managed for nine years. There was never a dull moment in this old building.

The first experience that I came aware of was told to me by one of my assistants. She and another employee were so shook up that they ran out of the business, locked the door, and then called the police. They saw these strips that hang down from shelves, moving back and forth as if someone had walked by them and bumped into them. They looked around and noticed all of them were moving. They called out to see if someone was in the building and did not receive an answer. Becoming nervous, that is when they left and called the police.

Two police officers arrived and the two women told them of their experience. The assistant unlocked the door to let them in so they could do a search. As soon as the officers went into the building, they thought they heard someone in the break room, so they made their way in there. Once in the room, they discovered there was no one there. They looked around satisfying themselves that the room was empty, they then walked out of the room. Almost immediately they heard footsteps going down an aisle. They split up thinking they would trap whoever it was between them. When they met up, neither had found anyone, and the footsteps were walking away from where they were standing.

They met back up with the assistant and the other worker, told them of their experience, and remarked that they didn't chase ghosts, and left.

My first experience in this building was when I was putting up some product on a shelf. I had someone up against my right ear and whisper my name. It startled me so much I fell into a shelf as if someone had pushed me! I felt the breath and pressure on and in my ear! That was the only time that I had that experience. Others have told me that have had that same experience.

I, along with my assistant, were stocking items on shelves when she asked me about a young girl, maybe twelve years old, was starring at her. I didn't think anything about it and kept working. A few minutes later, my assistant again told me about the girl just standing and watching her. I noticed the girl, and, indeed she was looking in the direction of my assistant. I joked saying maybe she thinks you are a ghost, and kept working. A few minutes later, my assistant said she was going to the break room for a minute. I asked if anything was wrong. She said she went down an aisle where a very young girl and her mother were shopping. The little girl looked at her, started crying, and hid behind her mother! Not knowing what was going on, she needed a break. I told her to take her time. It was strange, but, I think later on we figured out what was going on.

We believed we had a spirit of a little girl in the building. We don't know why and what happened, but the name, Anna, was used to identify her. A very good employee actually quit when she claimed to have seen the little girl peaking around a corner and looking at her. She said she shrugged it off the first time, but when it happened a second time, she couldn't handle it and left my employment.

Another employee was working a register when she noticed a balloon behind her. Since these balloons were filled with helium, she just figured it was leaking out some helium, which they do, and it needed to be refilled. She did that task and put it back in the balloon coral, where we kept them. Later on during the day, she turned around and that same balloon was behind her again. She laughed and went about her work.

Everywhere she went the balloon stayed behind her. Other workers and customers remarked how she had a balloon following her. After a while, the employee noticed the balloon was gone and when she looked for it, it was back in the balloon coral!

Now, you would think, end of story, just something weird with the helium, maybe static electricity, and the list could go on. Well, it's not the end of this story.

Around two years later, I had some workers come in to update the security system. They were putting in new cameras, alarm buttons, and other related items.

The first day, the supervisor was walking around the building to figure out how he and his crew were going to complete the project. A worker noticed that there was a balloon following behind the man. It continued to follow him down different aisles and into the office before someone mentioned it to him. He seemed surprised but not too concerned, he had a lot of work to do.

Day two for the man proved almost too much for him. He had taken over the office so he could run the new cables for all the cameras. He stepped out to check on what the rest of his crew was doing, and when he came back into the office, he discovered his tools were missing. He asked us if we had moved them, we replied no, we hadn't been in the office. He then asked everyone on his crew if that had moved them, they had also replied no. Frustrated, he went out to his truck to get more tools.

A few minutes later he came in with a strange look on his face. He had found his missing tools lined up neatly across the front seat of his truck, which was locked! He had the only key! I heard him mumble a remark that he couldn't wait to get the hell out of this spooky place!

There was another assistant that was closing one night.  She was completing the paperwork in the office when she heard the door knob to the office door start rattling.  She thought the co-worker closing with her was trying to scare her so she told her to stop.  A few minutes later it started again, so she looked at the security camera to catch her in the act.  What she saw was the co-worker was on the other side of the building.  The door knob was still rattling!  She hurried to finish the reports and left!

Another incident involving this same assistant involved the women's bathroom door.  She came to me and said that the door was locked.  She thought that someone was in there so she waited her turn.  After a period of time, no one came out, so she knocked on the door and received no reply.  She tried the door again, it was still locked.  I keep keys in the office just in case someone locks the door on accident when they leave.  After retrieving the keys I walked up to the door and when my hand touched the door knob, the door swung open!  The assistant, who was standing there the whole time, including when I went to get the keys, backed up and swore it had been locked.  She refused to use the women's bathroom and ended up going into the men's.

This next assistant was also in the office one night doing paperwork, when she heard someone beating on the wall.  The wall happen to be the one between the office and restrooms.  When the beating wouldn't stop, she left the office and went to the restrooms to see what

was going on and if someone needed help.  She found
no one.  Confused, she went back to the office and no
sooner had she sat down, the beating on the wall started
again!  She called the police!  The police arrived and
searched the! building but did not find anyone or
anything that could cause the noise.

I was sitting at home one evening when I received
a text from an assistant.  The text was, 'Anna is here,
lol'.  I didn't understand why my assistant would send
me that text.  Anna was also a name of a person who
worked for me, and I assumed the assistant was just
letting me know she had showed up to work.  Not sure
why she would do that unless the two of them were just
being playful.  I didn't reply, didn't feel it needed one.

The next day I mentioned the text I received to the
assistant, and she responded that she hadn't sent one.  I
pulled out my phone and showed her the text that came
from her number.  She was shocked!  She pulled out her
phone and there was no record of that text on her phone
sent to me.  She swore she didn't send it!  It then
dawned on us it might have been the little girl spirit we
called Anna, that sent it.  Really strange!  My assistant
would always talk about that text to several people
saying how it really shook her up.

There was many more odd things that occurred,
not only to us working in the store, but to customers and
vendors who came into the building.  Even had a truck
driver screaming because he saw a tall black figure

watching him and walking around his truck!  He was terrified and was visibly shaking.  When he left he said he would quit his job before he would come back!

Before I worked at this business, I had worked for another and it was also located in an old building.

The first incident I will discuss is when I cashier was talking to me and her scanner started beeping as if it was scanning merchandise.  We both looked at each other and figured it was the system doing a self re-set or something like that.  We continued our conversation when we heard it to continue to beep.  The cashier noticed that items were flashing across the screen!  There was nothing on the counter for it to scan.  After a few seconds a receipt printed and the cash drawer opened!  Somehow the scanner had scanned several items!  The register then completed the sale!  I called our technician and told him what had happened, and he just replied that it was impossible.  That night we were short in our deposit for the amount of that mysterious sale.  It never happened again.

One morning I had let the pharmacist in to go to his department, when we both heard a loud crash.  We walked over to where we thought the sound of the crash came from and noticed a large pile of framed art work in the center of the aisle.  I don't know how all the artwork could pile it self on top of each other, they were lined up down the whole aisle.  When I started cleaning up the mess, I noticed only the artwork that had religious

themes to it were damaged.  The rest of the art work
were not damaged!  Could be a coincident, I think not,
but I can't prove either way.

The stockroom was an interesting place.  A
worker had put together several new lamps and had
them stacked by one of the doors.  They were to be put
out the next day.
Everyone had left for the day and I was working on a
display on the sales floor, when I heard a terrific crash!
I thought about those lamps and thought that had fallen
and that would be a big mess!  Walking back to the
stockroom I was already dreading the mess I was going
to have clean up when I saw all the lamps lined up in a
row on a set of rollers!  The rollers are used to unload
the trucks.  How did the lamps go from next to the door
to lined up on rollers?  And, none were damaged!  What
was the crash I heard?  I looked everywhere and never
did find the source of the crash.

None of the workers liked being in the stockroom.
It just gave you a strange feeling.  Several people,
including myself, have heard voices, conversations,
while walking down a hallway to a private area.  This
occurred with me after the business was closed and I
was the only person in the building.  I heard what
sounded like two people having a conversation while
walking past me in that hallway.

When people would find out about my
background, they would wonder if something is

following me place to place.  Honestly, I don't know.  I have wondered that myself.

After working in both of these buildings for years, I can't help but wonder if there was a *demon next door!*

# Mother

These events occurred in my mother's house before she past away. Either I witnessed the event or my family did. Her house was built in the early 1900's and was when you had a parlor for the dead. The front of her house had two front doors. A lot of people always thought it was because it used to be a duplex. Not so. Houses built during this period had the two doors so when a family member passed, they would place them in the parlor. Visitors could then go thru the door that led to the parlor, pay their respects, then leave without having to interact with the family and bother them. The parlor of my mom's house was later made into a bedroom.

It was in this bedroom where some of the events would happen. I will start with mine. When I would come and visit my mom, my father had died many years previous, I would stay in this room. I lived around fours away.

I made it a point to make sure I opened the closet door before I got in bed and went to sleep. If not, I would hear knocks coming from within the closet! I have checked all thru that closet to see what it could possibly be, but was never able to figure it out. It never seemed to happen during the day, as far as I knew, but it did for sure at night. She didn't have rodents are any other infestation. I asked my mom about it and she just shrugged. Didn't seem to bother her. More on that later.

After spending a few weeks in the hospital due to an illness, my mother was ninety years old at the time, she was transferred to a facility for rehab. She still lived by herself and was very determined that she would continue to do so. I had a niece who was a nurse, and she would go by and check on her, as well as a home health nurse that would go by a few days a week. So, she always had someone nearby if she needed.

My daughter and her boyfriend went down to her house to spend the weekend cleaning and freshening up the house for her so when she got out of rehab she would have a nice and clean place to come back to.

The first evening my daughter called me and was worried. All of the dresser drawers were pulled out and left in the bedroom that used to be a parlor. I told her to check around the house to see if anyone may have broken-in while she had been gone. A few minutes later, she called back. Everything was fine, but while she was on the phone with me, somehow, the dresser drawers were pushed back in! It shook up her boyfriend so much, he slept on the floor by the front door and insisted all the lights be on!

One evening when I was sitting with my mother visiting, I asked her about the strange things that happen around her house.  She just nodded and told me that she knew of at least two spirits that were in the house.  It didn't bother her to have them there, in fact, they helped her.

She went on to tell me that she had fallen three different times during the last year, and she didn't want her doctor to know in case he would try and put her in a nursing home.  I reassured her that as a family, we had already decided that she would come live with one of us and we would not put her in a home.  I then asked who was in the house when she fell, she replied no one.  I asked how did you get up off the floor?  She had to use a walker to get around, there was no way she could get up off the floor without help. She just looked at me and smiled.  Never gave me an answer.  I knew then what she meant by the spirits in her home helping her!

We sold the house after her passing, and I often wonder if the people who bought the house are having any experiences.  I want to knock on the door and ask, but that in itself would be scary, don't you think?

# Cemetery

I try to go to a certain cemetery in the city I now live in, on veteran's day, to give my respect to those who served our country in the armed forces.  They have a very nice area where, if you are a veteran, you can be buried among your fellow veterans.  It is a large area, not sure how many acres, but a few.  A nice monument where they fly the flags of all the branches of the armed forces.  They have at least one person buried there that lost their life on 9/11.  All in all, a very nice place.

On one veteran's day visit, I had gotten out of my car and started walking among the graves.  When I do this, I talk softly saying thank you for your service as I go along.  After I had been there awhile, I went back to my vehicle to leave.  I don't know how to explain what happened next, other than I heard this voice in my head.  It told me to drive and it gave me directions on where to go.  I then had it tell me to stop.  This is a large cemetery and it had me drive to the other side of where I was, the veteran's area.

When I had stopped I got out of my vehicle and said, okay, now what?

The voice told me to climb a small hill towards a fairly large monument.  I did so, passing several graves on my way.  After reaching the top, I remember saying out loud, I am here for the veterans today.  The voice had me turn around and what I found was remarkable. In front of me, which would be the backside of two headstones, I read that those two individuals were veterans!

There was no way that you can read that from the road.  No flags or other decorations were on the graves to signify they were veterans.  No one would ever know of their service unless you actually walked up the hill and turned around to read it!

I thanked them for their service and for leading me to them.  Some things you just can't explain.

This obviously is not a demonic event, but I wanted to include it to show that if you leave yourself open, you may have something wonderful happen.  I consider this one of them.  I was honored to visit their final resting place.

# Ouija

A good friend of mine told me this story. I believe him because I have never known him to speak of something that wasn't true, and when he told me of this event, he became scared again. He wanted me to reach out to his family that was there and verify the incident. Knowing that it was a real event was important to him, and it was important that I knew, as well.

It happened at a family gathering at his house. Several members of his family were there, including high school aged kids. They were all enjoying being together and having a nice dinner. After dinner, the adults went into the living room to visit and relax, the kids went into his daughters bedroom to visit.

After about an hour, he heard his daughter screaming for help! He got up and ran to her bedroom. He tried to open the door, but it was locked. He yelled out to his daughter to unlock the door. All he heard in response was more screaming, this time from the other kids, as well.

He started beating on the door, all the time asking for someone to unlock the door. He was also asking what was going on. He kept hearing the words help us, help us!

Realizing that he wasn't getting in thru the bedroom door, he ran outside and around his house to get to his daughter's bedroom window.  When he looked inside he noticed all the kids running around the room and screaming for help.  There was nothing else to do, so he broke the window to gain access.

The kids then started crawling out of the window in sheer panic.  After they were out of the room, he went into the room.  The room was in a mess, the furniture had all been moved around, pictures were off the wall, and clothes were everywhere.  He couldn't figure out what they had been up to.

As he made his way to the bedroom door, to see what the problem was, it open easily.  He was now mad at his daughter and the rest of the kids.  He thought they were playing and wouldn't unlock the door because they figured it was a fun trick.

Once the kids were back in the house and settled down, he asked them what was going on?  The door opened without any problems.  He just had to break a window and now he was going to have to pay to fix it! He was not happy.

His daughter and the rest of the kids all promised that they were not playing a joke, the door would not open!

He asked why were carrying on by screaming and yelling for help?

The daughter told her dad that she was sorry, and led into the bedroom.  She started moving some of the things on the floor and uncovered the problem.  An ouija board!

The girl said that they started playing with it because they were bored and were curious.  At first, nothing happened.  Then, when they decided it was not going to do anything, they picked it up and tossed it in the corner.  They started laughing at it saying it was all make believe.

It was at that point the board flew across the room hitting one of the kids.  They started screaming and headed for the door.  The door would not open and they went into a panic.

Dad was mad that they had brought that into his house and told all of them in a not so peasant manner. The other adults agreed.

He then took the board, along with the other men who were there, and went out to his backyard and set it on fire to burn.

He swore to me, he and the others heard *screaming* coming from the board!

Another person had to come to his house to pick up what was left of it to take it off his property and throw it away.  He was too scared to touch it!

The following week he had his pastor come to his house to bless it.

I know that some people do not believe that the ouija board is anything and it is all in the imagination.  I myself have played with it and it didn't do anything.  It sits in a box under a table collecting dust.  Others say that it is a portal to another world or to demonic workings.  I personally cannot say, I have not had any bad experiences with one.

I have another friend, years ago, that had a bad experience.  He was playing with it by himself, and the planchette started moving across the board on its on.  It shook him up so much that he also took it outside and burned it.  And, he also said he heard screams coming from the board while it was burning.

That is two different people, years apart, that don't know each other and have never met, saying the same thing about what occurred when they burned the board.

Again, I have never personally had any bad experiences, but I know much has been written about them.  And, I haven't tried burning mine, either.

# Chapel

I had heard of this graveyard from several people and they all encouraged me to investigate.  It is an old with graves going back to the 1800's.  The small church is boarded up and hasn't been used for many years.  It is still well maintained and occasionally a new resident will be interred.  I don't think many more can be buried here, it appears to not have much room left.

My first trip there was during a nice summer afternoon.  I pulled up in the small parking lot and just sat for a few minutes taking in my surroundings.  It was a nice and quiet area.  Surrounded by trees, it appeared peaceful.

I was told of the stories of cars not starting, and having to be pushed out of the parking lot before they would run.  The sound of babies crying and shadow figures lurking around were also told to me.  A grave of a young girl whose father put a dollhouse on top, is said to have the spirit of the girl playing with her dollhouse.

Using this information, I set out to see what I could experience.  I walked the area and everything seemed peaceful.  I didn't feel like anything was out of place.

I went to take pictures of the graves of the children that bore the name of the graveyard, there were seven, and all had died as infants. These children are the ones that people have said they heard crying. My first picture took and I adjusted my stance to get another shot at a different angle and I noticed my camera stopped working. I looked it over and found that my battery was dead. I had just charged it that morning before making my trip. That was interesting. So, no more pictures that day.

I continued walking around and didn't have any other experiences that day.

As I was driving away I heard a pop sound coming from my camera. I stopped my car and looked to see what caused that noise. When I examined my camera, I noticed that my battery was back to fully charged! Okay, I guess I can add that story to the list.

A few months went by before I was able to make some time to go back. I wasn't disappointed.

I arrived and did what I normally due on an investigation. I again sat in my car and just took in my surroundings. This is such a peaceful place. Hard to believe all the stories I have heard.

After walking the area, I again didn't feel anything abnormal. As I walked past the chapel, I did hear what sounded like someone knocking from the inside.  I stopped to listen, and I heard it a few times more.  I walked around the chapel, it isn't very big, and it is completely boarded up with the doors padlocked and secured.  I stood there a little longer, and heard it two more times.  Just a steady knock of maybe three or four taps.  Never did figure out what that was.

Leaving, I said in a normal voice, I guess you are not feeling like letting me know you are here today.  I still wasn't convinced the knocking was paranormal.  So, I continued to my vehicle.  All of a sudden a very strong gust of wind came up and started sending leaves across the parking lot with a lot rush.  This lasted maybe ten seconds, then the wind died.  It was not windy that day and that was the only time it happened.  Not sure what you want to think about that.

I think a lot of what is experienced or the reputation that this graveyard gets, is from a little ways down the road from it. There use to be a small barn on an unpaved side road.  You had to climb a locked gate to get to it.  It was widely known some fifty years ago that this is where the local satanists would gather and have rituals.  It came complete with pentagrams, animal sacrifices, sex magic, and whatever else they get up to at these things.  The local farmer who owned the barn let them use it as long as they left him alone and did good luck rituals for him.  Apparently, the partnership worked out for them, he never complained.

The barn has long since been gone and nothing stands where it did, but people still like to go out to that area for the thrill of it, I guess.  The local satanic group have moved to another location, I will not say where, and they are still very active in this area.

They might be what you think is a *demon next door!*

# The Skull Lady

I really think you are going to like this one.  It is one of those stories that you know has to be true because I don't think anyone could make it up!

I was working one day in my office when a detective called me and said if I wasn't busy he needed me at a location where he would be serving a search warrant.  I was available so I got in my car and met him at the address he gave me.

When I first saw the house, I thought it may have been vacant, no curtains or blinds on any of the windows and what I could see looking thru them, not much furniture, either.

We went inside and the detective stated he needed the whole house photographed, and possible evidence collected, if any found.  He wanted to make sure I photographed showing the windows did not have any coverings.  I then completed what he asked.

While I was going around and taking my photographs of the house, I noticed some strange things. A woman lived in this home alone, and she had cat skulls placed everywhere.  There were two or three on the fireplace mantel, the end tables in the living room had at least two on each one.  The window ledges had at

least one of all of them.  In her kitchen I even found
them in the cabinets!  One was on her stove and another
in the center of her dining room table.  In her bedroom,
she had shelves all on the wall full of them.

Where did she get them all?  They looked cleaned
and well maintained.  She obviously took care of them.

The detective then called for me and I went back
into the ladies bedroom.  He wanted me to photograph
several shoe boxes of locust shells that he had found.
Also found was a copy of the satanic bible and another
book on satanic rituals.  This case is getting weird.  I
was about to find out how weird.

When I asked the detective what the case was all
about, he told me this.

The neighbors complaining about her is what
started everything.  They were upset because she liked
to walk around her house naked and dance.  That is done
a lot, I would imagine.  But, she doesn't have any
coverings over her windows and she liked to do the
naked dances at night with every light on in her house.

Word quickly spread, and there would be several
vehicles parked outside her house to enjoy the show.
This lady was very attractive, great figure, about twenty-
five years old.  As you can imagine, the neighbors didn't

appreciate all this traffic and eventually the empty beer cans and food wrappers in their yard from the audience.

So, hearing this, I didn't understand why a detective was involved, just should be handled by patrol. Well, it gets clearer.

This woman is a practicing satanist, and often had men over to her home to do sex magic rituals. Orgies is a better word.

During the search, we found several nude photos the woman had taken of herself in various poses, most had to do with her being crucified on a cross. It appeared she had blood on her in the pictures, but it could have been fake. I hope so. Not sure what those were for, but it may be something to do with her rituals.

Now, the reason the detective was given the case was that the woman claimed she had been raped. This is a very serious crime, and no matter what it should be investigated. I don't care who you are, you should never have this happen to you.

One night after dancing naked around her house, she heard a knock at her door. She answered the door, still naked, and saw a man on her porch. He pushed her back into the house and into her bedroom, where she was forced to perform oral sex. He left afterwards. She stated he never said anything to her and she had never seen him before.

While at the police department being interviewed, she opened her mouth and told the detective she had evidence for him.  She claimed she had pubic hair from the man stuck in between her teeth.  Thinking it was better to keep the hair in her mouth she wanted the detective to remove it.

When the detective asked her about the skulls, she just replied they give her energy for her rituals.  Where did she get them?  From various practitioners who were teaching her.  Were these people local?  Of course, we are everywhere!

I never heard if anything came out of this case. Just another mystery involving mysterious people.  I often wondered if she put a hex or curse on the man who raped her.

I do know that she moved out of that house shortly after this incident.  Maybe her neighbors encouraged her to do so.

The assumption is that her neighbors didn't know that they had a *demon next door!*

# Kill for Satan

Another ritual killing that has been stuck in my mind for these nearly thirty years since it occurred. A young lady living on drugs found herself with two men drunk with madness and a need to kill for Satan.

The two men in this case, who together, murdered this young lady, were known drug users. They would find themselves as drug dealers when the opportunities presented themselves, and when they were in need of money. Keeping normal jobs were something they were incapable of.

The victim, a beautiful young lady, just nineteen years of age, found herself hooked in the world of drugs and alcohol. She started meeting people that didn't have her best interests in mind. The spiral into this world became deeper and darker. She didn't realize some of these people were involved in a group that was making plans that involved her. Her days were numbered.

One of the suspects picked up the victim at a friend's house when he promised to get her high in exchange for sex. She agreed.

After arriving at the suspect's house, she noticed that the other suspect was there. She wasn't overly concerned but didn't expect him to be there.  She didn't like him, he was always aggressive and had a temper when drunk.

They settled down and begin drinking and taking drugs.  This went on for several hours into the early morning.  The suspect that had picked her up was ready to have sex with her so he took her into his bedroom.  She had hoped the other one would leave or a least pass out before she had sex, but that didn't seem like it would happen.

She noticed in the bedroom it was all decorated with some crazy stuff.  Pictures of the devil on the wall, candles around the bed, and what looked like horns above the bed on the wall.  They both undressed and they proceeded to have sex.  Afterwards, they drank some more and took more drugs.  The suspect she had just had sex with asked her to have sex with the other suspect, she refused.

After talking a bit more, he decided he wanted more sex with her and she agreed.  He wanted to tie her up and wanted her to act like he was raping her.  She agreed.  He tied her up to the bed face down.  He then started having rough sex with her.  She was complaining that he was too rough.  He became angry with her and started being more rough with her, hitting and slapping her.  She demanded he stop and untie her, she wanted to leave.  He told her she was never leaving.

When he gave his statement to the police, he said it was at this point he felt Satan started to talk to him. He had dabbled in satanism for awhile, but had never been too serious with it, until this night.

Satan had told him he needed to sacrifice this girl so he could realize his dreams and full potential.  So, while having sex with the victim, he started stabbing her repeatedly, crying out to Satan while doing so.  He had stabbed her over fifty times in the back.  The suspect claimed it was the best sex he had ever had.

After completing the sex act and killing the girl, he walked out of the bedroom naked with blood all over him.  The second suspect asked him what the hell was going on, and he told him he had sacrificed her to Satan. The other suspect stood up and went into the bedroom to see for himself.  After looking at the scene, and high on drugs and alcohol, he asked the first suspect if he could have a go at her.  He had always wanted to have sex with a dead body.

The first suspect told him to go ahead and do whatever he wanted.  The second suspect then went in and had sex with the dead girl.

After both men were done with the girl, they finally passed out on the living room floor.

The next day a friend of the suspects came by the house in hopes of scoring some drugs. When the door was opened by one of the suspects and let in, he was shocked at all the blood he saw. Both men were covered. He was trying to figure out what happened, did someone need medical attention, what was going on!

Both suspects were still groggy from the drugs and alcohol, and didn't really provide much information, so the concerned friend starting looking around. What he found in the bedroom made him physically ill. He ran out of the house and called for the police.

Police arrived to the horrific scene and found both suspects still in the house. They were subsequently arrested and taken to the police department for interviews. What I described is what they said had occurred. They didn't seem to have any remorse for what they had done to this poor girl. The suspect who actually did the killing was still saying that Satan was going to reward him and he couldn't wait.

The second suspect was arguing that he had done nothing wrong, the girl was already dead before he had sex with her, so he hadn't hurt her in any way. He wanted sex and her dead body was available.

Needless to say, both men were convicted and as far as I am aware, still in prison.  Not sure if the one ever received his reward from Satan, and if so, what it was.  I'm thinking he is probably still waiting.

Did the neighbors realize that they had a *demon next door?*

NB
OUIJA
NIO
AIBCDEFGHLJKKM
NOPQRSTUVWYY
12256799XYZ
XZ
ADSCST
NOR

# Oomancy

Most people have not heard of this.  It is a well used type of divination.  It is done by using an egg.  The egg is rolled over the body and later opened in a bowl.  If there is red within the egg, that meant that the practitioner was successful in removing 'evil' from your person.  Yes, you had to pay this person for their services.  People who thought they were given the 'evil eye' were the majority of users of this service.

This is another short story, and does not contain what we would call demons, but does contain what people will do to unsuspecting individuals who have a belief in a type of working that could possibly help them.  Con-artist, if you will.

I was contacted by a detective who was going to serve a search warrant at a residence that had a person performing oomancy.  This person has every right to do this, and individuals have every right to go to him to have this done, but, there was more to this story.

Upon entering the residence after announcing and identifying ourselves and presenting the warrant, I notice several people sitting in the living room.  Found out later the living room was the 'waiting area' until you were called.  Like a doctor's office.

The practitioner was in a bathroom, his office, with a 'patient'.  His co-worker was in the kitchen preparing eggs.

While we were waiting for the man to come out of the bathroom, I couldn't help but notice one of the women in the waiting room, a very beautiful Hispanic lady in her early 20's.  She was well dressed and did seem nervous with our presence.

I found out later she would come down to the police department and give a statement of her experience with this man.  It was enough to shut his operation down.

The man finally came out of the bathroom and he was told the reason we were there.  He seemed surprised, but told us to do what we needed.

I then photographed the house, especially the kitchen and the preparation of the eggs, and the bathroom.

An appointment was made for the man to come down to the police department where he could make a statement if he so desired.

We then left.

The man who was the practitioner never came in to talk to the detective, but the beautiful young lady I mentioned earlier, did.

In her statement she said that she had gone to see this man because her grandmother recommended it.  Her grandmother was a big believer in this area and said that her granddaughter needed it.

When we were there, she said that was her second time and she really didn't want to be there due to her first experience.  But, she was so convinced by what the man told her and then showed her red was in the egg, she felt she had to.

What made her go, besides her grandmother, was that she was starting to have problems at work, with her car, and finances.  Her grandmother believed that she had the 'evil eye' put on her and she needed it taken away.  That is when she told her about this man.

When she went, the living room was filled with other women waiting there turn.  That made her feel a little better.  If someone had this many people coming to them, they must be legit.

Nearly two hours went by before she was finally called back to see the man.  She noticed a woman in the kitchen with a lot of eggs on the table.

The man ushered her into a bathroom, which she thought was strange.  He then asked her why she was there.  She told him and he nodded his head agreeing with her grandmother, that someone had put the 'evil eye' on her.  He then told her she would have to do everything he instructed her to do, without question. She agreed.

He first had her turn in a circle slowly.  He then told her that he was going to take an egg and roll her all over her body.  She would have to take all of her clothes off for him to do so.  She wasn't comfortable doing that, but complied anyway.

He then started rubbing his hands on her body, telling her he was getting the flow going for the egg.  He massaged her breasts, rubbed her stomach, groped her buttocks, and inserted fingers into her vagina.

When done molesting her, he took the egg and rolled it all over her body.  He then cracked the egg in a bowl and it showed red inside it.  He then told her it was worse than he thought, which made her nervous and scared.

He then had her bend over a stool that was in the room, then proceeded to have sex with her.  She stated the sex lasted maybe twenty minutes.  During the sex, she didn't know what to do or say, she was shocked!

After finishing having sex with her, the man said that the sex was needed to prepare her body for the flushing.  She would need to do another appointment with him so he could do that.  But, what had been done on that day, should be enough for her to start seeing improvement in her life.

That was why we saw her on the day of the search warrant, she was there for her second appointment.

The detective asked her if she wanted to press charges against the man and she declined.  She was too embarrassed.

The detective went back to the house only to find it abandoned and empty.  The front door wasn't locked so he went in.  No furniture or anything else was found. It was obvious the man and woman had fled.

The detective started asking the neighbors about the man and woman, and they said they had moved in two or three months previous.  Within a week they started seeing cars and people going to the house every day.  They were concerned it might be drug related.

He then told the neighbors what had been going on and they were surprised and glad that they had left.

To some people, this had nothing to do with Satan or demons, but, I want you to consider how they were taking advantage of people thru fear and manipulation.

Not only were they taking money from them, but taking advantage of them physically for their own pleasure.

Some of those who claim to be able to do this practice, have been found to insert a red dye into the egg with a small needle.  Thus confirming the 'evil eye' to the unsuspecting victim.  We believe that is what the woman was doing in the kitchen the day we were there.

I believe you could call them a *demon next door.*